Aikido *complete*

Aikido *complete*

by Yoshimitsu Yamada

Photographs by Alexander Langfelder

The Citadel Press: *Secaucus, N.J.*

Fifth paperbound printing, 1981
Copyright © 1969 by Yoshimitsu Yamada
Published by Citadel Press
A division of Lyle Stuart Inc.
120 Enterprise Ave., Secaucus, N.J. 07094

In Canada: Musson Book Company
A division of General Publishing Co. Limited
Don Mills, Ontario

Manufactured in the United States of America by
The Book Press, Brattleboro, Vt.

ISBN 0-8065-0417-X

contents

此の度山田嘉光君が合気道の解説の本を出版する事に対し御悦びの言葉を述べたい。山田君は幼少の時より日本の合気道本部の内弟子として修行をし成長してからは本部部内各道場又本部近辺の各アメリカンキャンプにて合気道の指導に当り、語学の勉強もしてから、ニューヨークに赴任したのである。今、イーストコースト、フェデレーションのチーフインストラクターとして活躍中である。

滞米生活も三年以上になり、アメリカ人の指導に対し又独特の経験を持っている。「人を見て法を説け」という言葉がある。自分の好きな様に説明する事は易しいが、相手の人が理解出来ないのでは何もならない。相手の人によく理解させる様に説いてこそ、本当の説明である。

米人の気質をよく理解している山田君が合気道の根本原理に基いて彼等によく理解して頂ける様、此の度の出版は正しい合気道の普及に大いなる役割りを果すことを信じて疑わない。

合気道本部師範部長 藤平光一

I would like to congratulate Mr. Yamada on the publication of his first book on the art of Aikido.

Mr. Yamada was an apprentice at Aikido Headquarters in Tokyo since he was a boy. When he reached the status of instructor he began teaching at various Aikido schools and at all of the American military bases in the Tokyo area.

Partly because of this experience in teaching Americans, Mr. Yamada came to the United States in 1964 to become the head instructor at the New York Aikikai. He now, in addition, holds the important and very active position of Chief Instructor and President of the United States Aikido Federation. During these three years Mr. Yamada has increased his knowledge and understanding of the American people and gained important experience in teaching them. In Japanese, we have a proverb, roughly: One must first understand those he is trying to teach before he can be understood by or teach his students. I strongly believe that this book, which is based on the principles of Aikido, will do much to spread the art, helping people to understand the true meaning of Aikido.

KOICHI TOHEI
Chief Instructor of
Aikido World Headquarters
9th Dan in Aikido

When I came to this country to teach Aikido at the New York Aikikai, I found that my students came to Aikido for a variety of reasons: some for exercise and health, others to learn self-defense, and others to learn more about Oriental culture. However, after practicing together for awhile, they had only one goal: mastering the techniques and spirit of Aikido. When Aikidoists and students work together in the true spirit of this martial art, one can sense an atmosphere of peace and harmony, which in turn gives me great satisfaction, because I can feel that I have helped to contribute to the creation of this atmosphere.

Aikido has developed in the United States with remarkable rapidity. It was first introduced to the United States in Hawaii in 1953 by Professor Koichi Tohei, Ninth Degree Black Belt and Chief Instructor at Aikido General Headquarters in Tokyo. From Hawaii, Aikido spread to the west coast of the United States; but it was not until 1962 that an Aikido school was started in New York City. Although this first school in New York City began with a handful of students, today the New York Aikikai school of Aikido is a flourishing center from which Aikido is spreading throughout the eastern United States, and there are now Aikikais in Massachusetts, New Jersey, Long Island, and Florida.

More recently, Aikido training centers have been established in the Middle West as well.

Because of the growing interest in Aikido, I prepared this manual for the American public. Although the books by Professor Tohei and Professor Kishomaru Uyeshiba remain the standard works on Aikido, many practitioners have expressed a desire for a simple manual on Aikido written specifically for American students, particularly for those who do not live in an area where they can study in an Aikikai with a qualified instructor. I can not demonstrate all Aikido techniques in this book. I am currently working on another book, however, which will include additional Aikido techniques.

I would like to express my deepest appreciation for the inspiration and guidance I have received from Professor Morihei Uyeshiba, Master Kishomaru Uyeshiba, and Master Koichi Tohei. I am also grateful to Master Tohei for his permission to publish this book; to Lyle Stuart, the book's publisher and former president of the New York Aikikai; and to my students, whose help has made this work possible.

YOSHIMITSU YAMADA

August, 1969

Aikido *complete*

the
art
of Aikido

What is Aikido?

Aikido is a new Japanese martial art that has been developed by Morihei Uyeshiba. The main purpose of Aikido is to build a strong mind, body, and spirit for use in daily life. In addition, however, Aikido also trains its students to learn to live in harmony with themselves and with one another.

The Founder of Aikido

Morihei Uyeshiba developed Aikido. It is essential to know something about his life and work in order to appreciate the ideals and principles of Aikido. It was he who perfected the art of Aikido more than any other person. He must always be highly respected for it was he who went first, and the first person who explores some part of the wilderness of knowledge always has a harder task than those who follow him. In every dojo (school or club) there is a picture of Uyeshiba to show our respect for the founder.

Uyeshiba, who at this writing is eighty-seven years old and still teaching and giving demonstrations of Aikido throughout Japan, was interested in the martial arts even as a child. He studied and mastered many of them, such as various styles of jiu jitsu as well as sword- and stick-fighting. However, despite his achievement in these arts he felt that something essential was lacking. The mar-tial arts represented a way of life to him rather than merely a means of combat, and therefore they required a meaningful philosophy.

It was evident to Uyeshiba that today's victor will be defeated tomorrow, that the strong man will ultimately meet someone stronger and that pursuit of brute force must end in frustration. And no matter how fast one may be, there are limitations to physical capabilities.

Uyeshiba was filled with profound dissatisfaction with his achievements. He realized that his most formidable opponent was himself. The real purpose of the martial arts must be to purge oneself of petty ambitions and desires, to obtain control of one's own character before attempting to defeat others. Then, and only then, should one use his fighting ability, and then only in defense of that which is right, never for personal gain or ambition.

Uyeshiba discovered the spiritual potential of the martial arts. He believed that the basic principles of the universe are harmony and love and that these can be attained through the martial arts. He believed that a doctrine which does not teach these principles is not a true martial art. Still holding these beliefs today, he often expresses the idea that, from the perspective of the whole universe, our struggles, victories, and defeats are more than merely insignificant—they are non-existent.

The result of these concepts is Aikido, which Uyeshiba developed by combining all that he had learned from other martial arts with his new vision of the inner meaning and purpose of these arts. Over the years, Uyeshiba gradually has modified his original techniques and has added others.

It is easier to understand Aikido's underlying philosophy if one has had an opportunity to know Uyeshiba. I was fortunate enough to see him almost daily during my student apprenticeship. During that period I lived at the dojo headquarters in Tokyo, which was also Uyeshiba's home.

Despite his advanced age, Uyeshiba never missed the class he taught at 6:30 in the morning. Even when he felt ill he came to class; and the moment he stepped on the mat, he looked like a different person, years younger and filled with a very real strength. It seems to me that this can only be attributed to *ki*, an inner force which can transform a small, apparently frail old man into a youth capable of throwing any number of strong young men.

Contrary to one's preconceived mental picture of a master of the martial arts, Uyeshiba is always serene and smiling. His eyes are piercing; yet, at the same time, they have a very calm, kind quality about them. If he had aimed in the martial arts only to achieve strength to defeat others, I do not believe he could have developed such a peaceful mien. His inner calm immediately affects others when they come in contact with him. One always feels much more at peace when in his presence.

Uyeshiba's most outstanding characteristic is his modesty. He frequently says that he himself is only a student of Aikido, practicing diligently in order to open the way for others. Since for him Aikido is a way of life, there can be no end to one's apprenticeship. This is something that all of us who practice Aikido should always keep in mind. It should stimulate us to keep practicing in the spirit of students, in all modesty, for if Uyeshiba still considers himself a student of Aikido, then what are we?

The Techniques of Aikido

Aikido techniques employ circular rather than linear movements, with the defender's moving out of the line of attack and then using his opponent's own momentum to overcome him. The defender does not attempt to block his opponent's blows or in any way to clash with his opponent's force. Instead, he "leads" his opponent's power and mind. Thus, it is essential for the student to learn to sense the direction of his attacker's power in order first to avoid it and then to use it.

This is why it is impossible to learn Aikido without practicing with another person and why a certain harmony must exist between the partners who are learning Aikido together. The student must learn to understand his opponent's—or, in training sessions, his partner's—feeling, and until one develops this sensitivity, he cannot "lead" another's mind or, consequently, his power.

There is no contest of brute force in Aikido, nor does Aikido employ striking or bone-breaking techniques. To illustrate: In Aikido when various wrist locks are applied, the wrist is bent in the direction it goes naturally, never in the opposite direction. In my opinion, wrist locks and other joint techniques are no more than forms of practice. To a beginner they seem to be the ultimate in effectiveness and devastating when used against an opponent, but to me they are only methods to strengthen and prepare one's self. The practice of such techniques forms and develops the student, and when he has achieved a certain proficiency, his opponent cannot find a good opportunity to attack.

Aikido, as it has been developed by Morihei Uyeshiba, does not have as its primary goal the defeat and injury of one's opponent. Rather it is designed to remove the idea of aggression from the antagonist's mind by yielding to his force in such a way that he hurts only himself with his aggressiveness. Therefore, Aikido is strictly defensive—*there are no competitive contests between Aikidoists*. To practice Aikido, one's partner must use some form of attack to which an Aikido defensive technique is applied. The mental attitude that is cultivated during Aikido practice is one of relaxed alertness in which no thought of conflict or competition is allowed to interfere with one's instantaneous response to attack.

This mental attitude is very important. I will pursue it in greater depth when I discuss the concept of *ki* but the student must always bear in mind that although training the body is important, training the mind is even more so.

Some people concentrate solely on the physical aspect of training. But it is possible that even if they study the martial arts for many years, when suddenly attacked on the street, they may forget their training and be unable to defend themselves with even the most elementary technique because they are in a mental state of confusion and tension. It is only by constant discipline of his mind that one is able to preserve an inner calmness that permits an immediate and effective reaction in the face of emergency.

As part of his training, the Aikido student always tries to practice in a composed, alert state, which enables him to turn his attention rapidly from one attacker to another. His mind must have the flexibility to cope with new situations without being preoccupied with past ones. Possession of this faculty is invaluable: Not only does it help one to meet life's day-to-day problems, but also in defense situations it empowers him to be particularly effective against attack by more than one assailant. When I give Aikido demonstrations, I have noticed that the situation which most impresses, but at the same time most bewilders, onlookers is when I defend myself against a number of men attacking me at the same time. Often the spectators can hardly believe that the attack and the defense are spontaneous and unrehearsed.

Yet such a defense is possible, due to the mental and physical training that I have briefly described. A well-trained Aikidoist can defend himself against many men, because in training he always tries to be aware of the *entire situation* and not to concentrate on just one element. When I am practicing with one partner I do not concentrate solely on the wrist, for example, which I may be holding, but on all of him. And when attacked by more than one man, I am aware not only of my immediate opponent, but of all the others as well.

Concentration on the One-Point

Before the Aikido student can begin to practice the actual Aikido techniques, he must know how to coordinate his body and mind. He must first learn how to keep what is called the "one-point." This is a hypothetical point located 2 inches below the navel, which is considered the center of the body's gravity. By relaxing the body and concentrating the mind on his one-point, even when he is moving, the student is able to achieve perfect balance and mental stability while executing the most difficult movements.

At first this is very difficult, but the student should try to keep his mind on the one-point during all of his daily activities, not just while he is practicing on the mat. With this constant mental discipline, the student will find that he will ultimately be able to achieve this concentration easily, without making a conscious effort.

It can't be emphasized sufficiently that relaxation is very important. Most participants, when facing an opponent, become very tense, tightening their muscles and hunching their shoulders. This position may appear strong, but it is really very vulnerable, because all of the defender's strength is concentrated in the upper part of his body. In Aikido we would say that when a defender in this position is pushed on the shoulder, his one-point moves up; that is, his mind is concentrated on the upper part of his body and, therefore, he loses balance. Moreover, it is impossible to maintain such a tense position very long, because it is so tiring. However, if a person is pushed on the shoulder while he is relaxed, he is able to absorb the pressure and thus is able to react more flexibly, using his opponent's power. One is able to cope with a sudden attack only when he has learned to keep himself relaxed and alert at all times.

These principles are vital to many other activities. Baseball players have told me that they are only able to bat well if they are properly relaxed and "stand low" in their batting stance. Then, they say, they are able to swing quickly and that no matter what kind of ball is pitched, when it reaches the plate there is a second when it seems to stand still. But this is so only if they are not tense and off-balance. Dancers also have told me that they must "think low" and relax in order to keep their balance while executing rapid turns and other difficult movements; and for this reason we have many dancers studying at the New York Aikikai.

Keeping the one-point also has beneficial effects on other aspects of life. In our tense, busy existence we tend to become upset easily over the most insignificant matters. However, if we maintain our one-point at all times, we are always serene, even under the most trying circumstances. I have been told by my students that in the midst of tense business meetings they have tried consciously to keep their one-point and have found that not only were they more relaxed and less likely to become ruffled, but also they were able to see the situation under discussion more clearly and comprehensively. Also they were able to understand and appreciate other points of view more readily. Previously, they tended to see only one side of a question, and hence were dogmatic and less flexible. This ability to understand one's opponent and to put one's self in his position is very important in Aikido.

The accompanying photographs illustrate the above tenet. In *Photo 1* I clenched my fists and tensed my upper body. Of course, I could not keep my one-point in this position and this permitted my opponent to lift me easily. But in the second picture I relaxed and let all of my weight settle in my body by concentrating my mind on my one-point. In this position I was not subject to my opponent's power as he tried to lift me but found me too heavy. However, whenever I cease concentrating on my one-point, I become aware of my opponent's power and think that he can lift me; and he is then able to do so (see *Photo 2*).

The student must believe and be absolutely convinced that his weight has dropped into the lower part of his body or else his attention will wander and he will be overcome. This conviction will only evolve from experiencing the feeling repeatedly through actual practice. Many times, as I am describing Aikido methods, I will emphasize that *you must control your one-point* in order for the techniques of Aikido to be effective.

Understanding and Control of the *Ki*

The next objective is how to use one's own power most effectively, and this involves the concept of *ki*. It is practically impossible to translate the word literally into English because it means many things in Japanese.

Ki is the power of the spirit or the mind that we all possess but which we use only on rare occasions. Aikido teaches us to use it often and at will. In emergencies we are all capable of reacting extraordinarily. We are able to accomplish such acts during stressful situations because we draw on inner reserves of strength and energy. In Aikido we try to learn how to summon this energy at will and apply it not only to our martial techniques, but eventually and through practice, also to all phases of our daily life. The aim of an Aikidoist is to control this power in such a way that it will flow naturally whenever it is needed.

But *ki* has other meanings. When someone attacks us it might appear that his fist is the first thing to reach us. However, before an assailant throws his punch, he has already thought of attacking us and has turned his mind entirely to this idea. We say that he is extending his *ki* toward us when he does this, and it is by training ourselves to feel this mental force that we are able to respond to his attack *before* it has been launched. And in our techniques, we try to "lead" an opponent's *ki;* that is, to lead his mind and power in order to overcome him.

Ki can also be defined as the coordination of mind and body. If we direct our mind in a certain area, our whole body follows it naturally. However, if we have

Photo 1

Photo 2

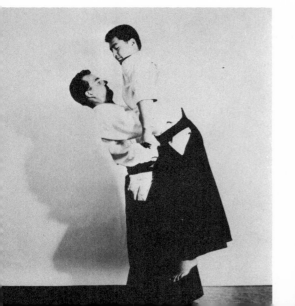

decided to go in one direction but attempt to move in another, we find ourselves moving clumsily. Nothing is more powerful than when our mind and whole body function in coordination.

Again, this concept can be understood more easily by studying an illustration. As *Photo 3* demonstrates, my opponent is bending my arm easily. My arm *looks* strong because I have clenched my fist and am using all of the power in my arm to resist my antagonist; but actually my arm is weak. I am very tense and am not keeping my one-point; now it is just a contest of force in one area of the body, and the stronger man will prevail.

In *Photo 4* I have relaxed my arm and whole body by keeping my one-point, and at the same time I am thinking that my power is extending through my arm to my fingertips. I concentrate on my conviction that my power is constantly going out into the distance and that my arm is unbendable, that my opponent is unable to bend my arm. And yet my arm is so relaxed that I am able to move my hand from one side to the other even while he is trying to bend my arm with all his strength. However, the second I stop thinking that my power is flowing through

my arm, it will bend. This is what we call the *extension of ki*. In Aikido we feel that our power must be constantly extended because otherwise our power will stop short and we cannot lead our opponent's power, or *ki*.

The concept of leading our opponent's *ki* is fundamental to all Aikido techniques. If we simply extend our power toward our opponent and he extends his toward us, then we will clash, and again it will be only a contest of strength. Therefore, we learn to sense the direction of his power, or *ki*, and we move out of the way and lead his power by joining our *ki* with his. This is a very simple principle that we constantly apply.

In some of our techniques in which we use an "entering" (*irimi*) movement rather than a "turning" (*tenkan*) movement, it seems as though we are blocking the blow and clashing with our opponent's force, but in reality this is not so. As will become evident from the following explanation of Aikido techniques, an Aikidoist does not block his opponent's blow, but rather *avoids* its force, deflecting and leading it in order to throw his opponent.

Photo 3

Photo 4

demonstration and explanation of the techniques and philosophy of *Aikido*

Now I would like to demonstrate some of the techniques of Aikido and explain how they should be practiced. These are basic skills. There are many more than the ones described in this manual, but they cannot be accomplished until these basic forms are mastered. Inasmuch as there are several different forms for each attack and although one may have absorbed all of these, frequently it may be necessary to improvise beyond the basic methods. All Aikido techniques are flowing and continuously moving motions, and they cannot be stopped at any time. If in your practice you feel yourself being stopped, it is because you are not applying the art correctly.

In these pages you will find constant repetition of the belief that in practice one must never compete. This can't be stressed enough. One must concentrate solely on the technique, nothing else. Also, remember that Aikido offers much more than self-defense. It is a way to train your mind and body so that you can live a happier life.

There are no specific rules governing Aikido in actual combat. There are rules covering practice sessions, but these are only for the purpose of developing one's skills in the "classroom" approach. One must be able to react spontaneously to each new situation as it arises. Always remember that Aikido is a purely defensive art and that it should never be used aggressively or to hurt someone unnecessarily. There is no room in Aikido for the bully.

For the beginner it is also important to remember not to try to overcome his "assailant" but rather to help him learn the Aikido techniques. You are not fighting each other in Aikido—you are trying to learn. When you become an advanced student, you may ask your "attacker" to resist you, but there is real danger in doing this too early in your training. The danger is that you may substitute force for dexterity.

How to Fall

I must stress the importance of the proper method of falling, or, as they say in Japanese, *ukemi*. *Ukemi* dissipates the fear of falling and reduces the danger of

Photo 5

Photo 6

injury. There are times too when *ukemi* becomes a definite defensive move that can leave an attacker quite surprised.

Photo 5. In this exercise you are going to roll on your left side. First, put your left foot forward with the leg bent from the knee. Next, put your left arm around and under your left knee, and reach for the mat with your hand. Do not yet put your weight on your arms. Prepare to fall by concentrating on keeping your left arm unbendable and circular. Most important, make sure that you keep your arm unbendable *all the way through the roll* until you regain your footing. The right arm should remain relaxed and close to the body all the time. You should put your head down, close to your chest so that it will not strike the mat. A good way to help you keep your head close to

your chest is to watch your waist until you rise, at which time you must look directly ahead to help you up.

Photo 6. In this picture, the Aikidoist is about to roll by kicking off with his right foot. If you are afraid to roll, you become stiff and will not roll roundly. Try to form your body into a ball so that you will roll softly and quietly. Notice that the body is almost a complete circle from the hip to the left arm and that the Aikidoist is trying to push his left hand to his left heel.

Photo 7 shows the Aikidoist as he lands on the mat. In *Photo 8* he regains his standing by using his right knee and putting his left foot forward. Notice that his left arm is in exactly the same position as when he started.

The Shiho-Nage Technique

Photo 9 shows the key position of Shiho-Nage. In this picture Uke (the attacker) is about to be thrown. Nage (the one who throws the attacker) holds Uke's wrist with both hands, and then brings Uke's wrist straight down.

Photo 9

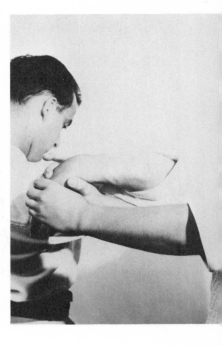

KATATE-TORI SHIHO-NAGE, *Irimi* MOVEMENT *Irimi* is the Japanese word used to show that the technique is an "entering" one. An *irimi* method is one in which the defender moves *toward* his attacker. *Photo 10* shows the starting position. Uke (the attacker) holds Nage's (the defender's) wrist; to defend himself, Nage will apply Shiho-Nage to Uke. Nage should point the fingers of the hand that Uke is holding in the direction he intends to move; at the same time, Nage should extend his *ki*. Unless Nage points his fingers and extends his *ki*, he will be stopped when he moves his left foot, as shown in

Photo 10

Photo 11

Photo 11. If Nage closes his fingers, all of his *ki* will stop in his fist, and as a result he will not be able to lead Uke's power. If Nage stops the flow of *ki*, he will be unable to properly execute the form and will resort to force. As indicated earlier, this will be successful to some degree only on those weaker than he.

To avoid using force, Nage should remember to keep his fingers pointing in the direction he wishes to go and to keep his shoulders loose. Nage should also keep his arm bent circularly, so that when he steps the whole movement will become circular. (In Aikido 80 per cent of the movements are circular.)

As shown in *Photo 12,* Nage starts his move by putting his left foot forward. At the same time, Nage lightly but firmly takes hold of Uke's right wrist and brings both arms upward. Notice that Nage still

Photo 12

Photo 13

extends his fingers and brings his whole arm upward so that he has enough space to pivot (his next movement). If his arm is too low, he cannot hold Uke's wrist easily. Nage's arm should be under Uke's. When Nage holds Uke's wrist, he should not hold too tightly. If he does, Uke will feel pressure and pull his arm back in a reflex action.

Nage is about to pivot, as shown in *Photo 13*. At this point, Nage keeps his whole body low, bending both knees slightly and keeping Uke's arm close to his head so that Uke cannot pivot to escape. Nage still holds Uke's wrist gently. Notice that Nage's left fingers are still pointing in the direction he leads, and that both of Nage's feet are pointed outward. This helps Nage to keep his balance. *Photo 14* shows how Nage should stand after he pivots. Nage should continue the motion all the way through to the finale

Photo 14

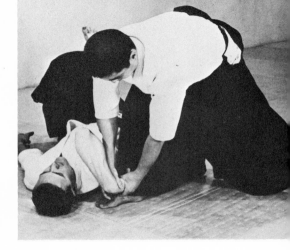

Photo 15

of this move.

However, it is important here to describe Nage's proper position. First, Nage should pivot completely and then stand almost straight. His right foot should point outward to keep his balance. Nage holds Uke's wrist tightly but should not stiffen his shoulder; if he does, all of his power will concentrate in his shoulder, making it difficult for him to swing both arms down. Both arms should be straight

so he can swing them vigorously. He should keep Uke's wrist directly in front of him to concentrate all of his *ki* and power on Uke's wrist (see again *Photo 9*). Then Nage brings Uke's wrist down toward his right foot.

Photo 15 shows the finale of this move. As Nage brings Uke down, he may have to slide his right foot forward, depending on how both Nage and Uke are positioned in relation to each other.

KATATE-TORI SHIHO-NAGE, *Tenkan* MOVEMENT   Most of Aikido has two kinds of movements: *irimi* and *tenkan*. I have explained *irimi;* now I would like to describe *tenkan*. This is the method by which Aikido becomes graceful and smooth. As I discussed before, most Aikido movements should be circular. In the demonstrations presented here, Nage stays in the center of the hypothetical circle in which they practice and leads Uke around him. If Nage moves, Uke is forced to move two or three times farther than Nage, which gives a decided advantage to Nage. *Tenkan* means "to pivot," and when you pivot you lead your opponent circularly before you apply any of the attendant skills.

In *Photo 16*, Nage is planning to apply Shiho-Nage, using the *tenkan* movement. Nage and Uke face each other; Nage should lead Uke by facing in the same direction as Uke. Unless Nage does this he must pull Uke toward him. Thus, both would be fighting each other, and if Nage pulls his hand, naturally Uke will also pull. Instead, Nage bends his wrist to make both their powers shift in the same direction. At this point it is very important for Nage to extend his *ki* positively and keep his shoulders relaxed. After both powers have met at Nage's wrist, they will flow in the same direction. If Nage does not extend his *ki,* he will receive all of Uke's power and be unable to move or lead Uke.

After Nage places himself in the proper position, he is ready to execute the movement see *Photo 17*). When Nage moves, he doesn't have to be concerned about his hand since he leads Uke's power in the direction initiated by Uke. Since Uke holds only Nage's wrist, Nage's body is otherwise completely free. But as often happens to beginners, as soon as they are

Photo 17

Photo 16

Photo 18

Photo 19

Photo 20

held by the wrist, all their attention is concentrated on that one area where they feel their opponent's power. Thus, they can hardly move because they will lose their balance easily. In other words, because they concentrate only on a lesser situation, they cannot see the whole setup. To repeat our important rule, the Aikidoist should always keep in mind that the center of mind and body is 2 inches below the navel (the one-point).

In *Photo 17,* Nage twists his hip. At the same time he should turn his face. The face and fingers should point in the same direction and he should never look at Uke. After he pivots, his left leg should be bent. In *Photos 18* and *19,* Nage puts his right foot back after he twists his hip. Now Nage stands next to Uke and is ready to lead. Notice that Nage's face and fingers are still facing the same direction and that his left arm is circular. In *Photo 20,* Nage leads Uke's arm in front of him to hold Uke's wrist. Following this position, the method is the same as shown in *Photos 13, 14,* and *15.*

Photo 21

Photo 22

YOKOMEN-UCHI SHIHO-NAGE, *Irimi* MOVEMENT *Photo 21* shows the starting position. Uke is about to hit Nage's neck and Nage will catch Uke's wrist to apply Shiho-Nage. Nage can accomplish this even if Uke holds a weapon. Uke attacks Nage's left side. Nage is standing in left *hanmi* (his left foot forward). As shown in *Photo 22*, Nage puts his left foot back as Uke comes forward, blocking Uke's blow with his left hand; with his right hand, Nage strikes at Uke's neck. Nage's left arm should be unbendable. He

should not try to hold Uke's wrist at this time since he is apt to concentrate only on that area and will probably forget to step back. This would likely cause Nage to lose his balance, especially if Uke's blow is firm. But by the technique suggested Nage will take all of Uke's power. Then, cutting Uke's right arm down with his unbendable left arm, Nage simultaneously slides his right hand along and inside Uke's right arm to Uke's wrist, holding the latter lightly. At the same time, Nage draws his right leg back to main-

Photo 23

Photo 24

Photo 25

Photo 26

tain balance, but should not put his weight on it because he has to move it in the next motion. Nage should keep Uke's arm directly in front of him and face Uke (*Photo 23*). Uke loses his balance because Nage did not stay where Uke concentrated all his power.

Photo 24 shows the most important part of this technique. Nage lifts Uke's right arm with both hands, with a twisting motion. Nage should not push Uke's arm toward Uke; their arms should be straight so that Nage has plenty of room when he

pivots. Nage also twists his hip as he lifts Uke's arm, and faces in the direction to which he is shifting. Nage may put his right foot to his right side when he twists his hip if he finds it necessary. Notice that Nage turns his foot to the outside. This facilitates keeping his balance when he pivots. Nage's next move is to position his left foot and then to pivot. Explanations for *Photos 25, 26,* and *27* are the same as for *Photos 13, 14,* and *15.*

Photo 27

Photo 28

Photo 29

YOKOMEN-UCHI SHIHO-NAGE, *Tenkan* MOVEMENT Uke attacks in the same manner as he did in the last method. In *Photo 28*, Uke makes a fist but that doesn't intimidate Nage. *Photos 28 29*, and *30* are the same movement as *Photos 21, 22,* and *23·*

In the last *irimi* (entering) movement, Nage put his left foot forward, following the position of *Photo 30*, but here Nage makes the *tenkan* (pivot) movement. In

30

Photo 30

Photo 31

Photo 32

Photo 33

Photo 31, Nage places his left foot next to Uke's right. At this point, Nage should extend his arms. (*Photo 32* is taken from the opposite side of *Photo 31*.) As Nage positions his left foot, he should not look at Uke. If he does, he will probably lose his balance and they might crash into each other. They should both face in the same direction. After the movement shown in *Photo 31*, Nage puts his right foot back and is thereby in the pivoting position.

Before he pivots, Nage lifts Uke's arm to facilitate his pivot. The technique must be executed in one motion, from *Photo 30* through *33*. In short, Nage's left and right steps should be executed very swiftly. As soon as he turns, Nage brings his arm down. In *Photos 34* and *35*, Nage is completing this technique. He may have to move forward as Uke falls, and he should keep his right foot forward to the conclusion.

Photo 34

Photo 35

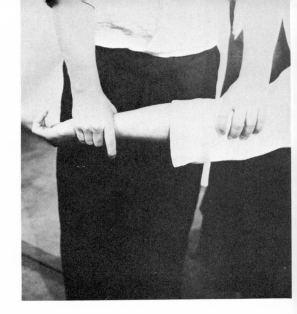

Photo 36

The Ikkyo Technique

Ikkyo is one of the basic skills of Aikido. Nage holds Uke's arm, as in *Photo 36*, and secures Uke to the mat. Nage places his left hand on Uke's elbow and holds the wrist with his right hand. Both of Nage's arms should be straight as he extends his *ki* in the downward direction he intends to take Uke. If his right arm is lower than the left (the one on Uke's elbow), all of Nage's power is directed at Uke's wrist, and all of his effort is consequently dissipated.

SHOMEN-UCHI IKKYO, *Irimi* MOVEMENT
Shomen-Uchi is a means of attack. Uke strikes at Nage's forehead. It is as if Uke had a weapon. *Photo 37* shows the starting position of this technique. It's important for Nage to anticipate Uke's blow. In *Photo 37*, Nage is awaiting Uke's attack. As Uke's blow descends, Nage brings both his arms up and puts his left arm under Uke's elbow. Notice that in *Photo 38*, Nage does not grasp Uke's wrist. His right fingers point up, and he extends his *ki;* both powers are led in the same direction when they meet. *Photo 39* shows the incorrect approach to this technique: Here Nage did not extend his *ki* and

Photo 37

Photo 38

Photo 39

thus received the full force of Uke's power.

Nage leads upward and will make a circle in front of Uke's face. This means that their powers are not fighting. If Nage tries to push Uke's arm toward Uke's face or if Nage tries to grasp Uke's wrist, he can hardly push Uke back, especially if Uke is very strong, because he is fighting against Uke's power instead of harmonizing with it.

Photo 40 shows half of this circular movement. Nage grasps Uke's wrist while he makes the circle; and as he twists his hip to the right, he turns his right foot to the right. By turning his foot out-

Photo 41

Photo 40

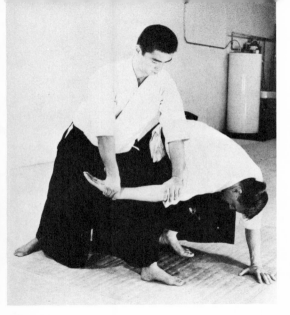

Photo 42

Photo 43

Photo 44

ward, it is easy for him to keep his balance and to twist his hip. When Nage makes the circle, he must not extend too far, because this might cause him to lose his balance. Nage has completed the circle in *Photo 41*. He does not hold Uke's arm too tightly because doing so would cause his *ki* to be arrested at his hands. Nage puts his left foot forward (*Photo 42*). While he steps forward, he should extend his *ki* downward and keep walking until Uke falls (*Photo 43*). *Photo 44* is the conclusion of this form. Nage places both knees on the mat with his left knee close to Uke's armpit and pins Uke to the mat with *ki*. Uke cannot rise.

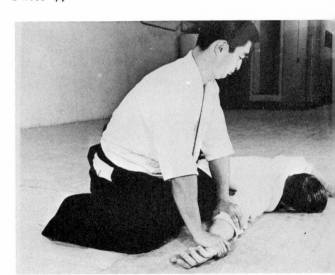

SHOMEN-UCHI IKKYO, *Tenkan* MOVE-
MENT Nage stands with his right foot
forward facing Uke (*Photo 45*). As Uke
approaches, Nage brings both arms up,

Photo 45

extending his *ki* (*Photo 46*). This is almost the same as the beginning of the
previous form, but in this (*tenkan*) movement, Nage does not go forward. As
shown in *Photo 47*, extending both arms,
Nage puts his left foot behind Uke. Nage
should not step too close to Uke, because
he will not have sufficient room to extend
his arms. If Nage's arm is bent, he will
have difficulty when he pivots on his next
move. This situation is depicted in *Photo
48.* Here Nage is pulling Uke's arm and
having difficulty. He should have kept
both arms down. In this instance, his *ki*
is limited to Uke's arm, and consequently
the whole movement stops.

Photo 49 shows the proper position following that shown in *Photo 47*. Notice
that Nage's arms are straight and his *ki*
is extending to the mat through Uke's
arm. Nage should keep Uke's arm directly
in front of him as he pivots; and while

Photo 46   *Photo 47*

his body is moving circularly, Nage should extend both arms downward. He should never pull at Uke's arm. Nage looks in the direction at which he aims. Since Nage is taking Uke downward, he has to go down also while he is pivoting. Nage's inside knee (left, in this case) should land first (see *Photos 50* and *51*).

Photo 48

Photo 49

Photo 50

Photo 51

YOKOMEN-UCHI IKKYO, *Tenkan* MOVE-MENT Yokomen-Uchi is a form of attack.

In *Photo 52,* Uke is about to hit the left side of Nage's head, as Nage stands facing him with his left foot forward. Nage should not wait for Uke's blow. If Nage waits, he will receive all of Uke's power and he will become immobile, as illustrated in *Photo 53.* Before Uke comes toward him, Nage should slide in the direction of Uke, as shown in *Photo 54.* This is the most important part of this movement. If Nage slides in strongly enough to push Uke back it becomes another technique of Aikido. As Nage slides, he moves diagonally away to place himself almost alongside Uke. He should not put his right foot forward as he enters. His left foot is still forward and his legs are bent to keep his weight low. This facilitates balance. Very often beginners, while sliding wrongly, will block their opponent's arm, causing their whole weight to come up and thereby losing their balance. Again, to repeat, the Aikidoist should remember to concentrate on the one-point.

In this exercise, when Nage slides, both arms should be unbendable, and Nage should keep his left arm circular but only *slightly* bent.

In *Photo 55,* Nage grasps Uke's wrist with his right hand and slides his left foot to Uke's back. While Nage holds Uke's wrist, he moves his left hand to Uke's elbow, pivoting backward on his left foot. Nage's arms should be straight all the way until he finishes pivoting. The movements shown in *Photos 56, 57,* and *58* are the same as the concluding forms of the Shomen-Uchi Ikkyo *tenkan* movement described earlier.

Photo 52

Photo 53

Photo 54

Photo 55

Photo 56

Photo 57

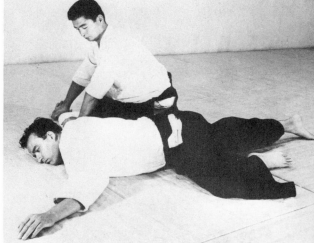

Photo 58

Photo 59

KATATE-TORI RYOTE-MOCHI IKKYO, *Tenkan* MOVEMENT Uke grasps one of Nage's arms with both hands, and Nage applies the Ikkyo technique to Uke. No matter what technique Nage applies against this attack, he must move to unbalance Uke. In *Photo 59,* Uke holds Nage's arm firmly, preventing Nage from applying any technique unless Nage leads Uke to the direction of his *ki.* In this case, Uke does not pull Nage toward him, but rather, he extends his *ki* forward, and Nage moves to Uke's side to lead Uke around him as shown in *Photo 60.* In any Aikido movement, Nage never stands in Uke's way when he leads Uke. As Nage pivots, he relaxes the arm that Uke holds (in this demonstration, the right arm).

Photo 60

Photo 61

If his arm is rigid, a contest of force will ensue at the point where their powers meet, and Nage will have great difficulty moving. When Nage pivots, if he maintains a relaxed arm, his elbow goes down naturally and his fingers point up. It is important to point the fingers up because Nage will want to lift Uke. As he pivots, Nage should turn his face and his body in the direction he intends to lead; he should not look at Uke. If he does, his mind stops on Uke, and both Nage's and Uke's movement will stop.

Photo 61 shows the crucial part of this technique. After Nage leads Uke from the position of *Photo 60*, he intends to change his position to the other side of Uke. The circle will move as Nage moves; Nage is the center of the circle. Before Nage puts his left foot to Uke's right side, he should twist his hip, while cutting his right arm down to his right side. As Nage cuts down with his right arm, he should not push Uke's arm violently toward Uke. Nage's left arm is about to reach Uke's elbow. Nage has put his left foot to Uke's right side in *Photo 62* and is about to start the final pivot, bringing Uke's arm down to his right side. Nage keeps both arms straight (*Photo 62*) and puts his right foot back, as shown in *Photo 63*. Nage is not looking at Uke. If Nage's left foot is in Uke's way when he pivots, he may move his foot away and keep pivoting until he can fasten Uke to the mat (*Photo 64*).

Photo 62

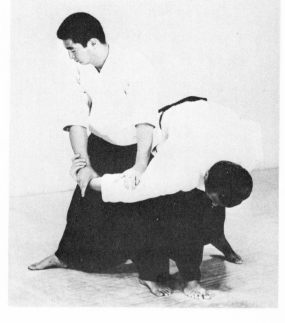

Photo 63

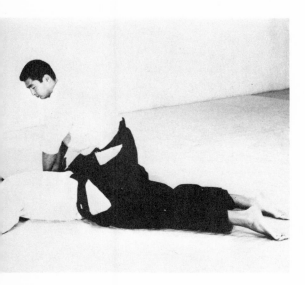

Photo 64

The Nikkyo Technique

This is the most painful technique of Aikido and if not executed properly, serious injury can result. *Photo 65* shows how to hold the opponent's wrist properly for the Nikkyo technique.

Photo 65

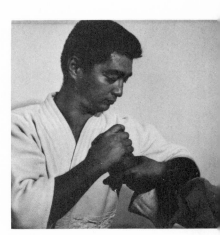

SHOMEN-UCHI NIKKYO, *Tenkan* MOVE-
MENT Uke strikes at Nage's forehead
and Nage grasps Uke's wrist and applies
Nikkyo (*Photos 66* and *67*). As Uke approaches, Nage blocks the blow with his
right arm and grasps Uke's wrist with his
left hand. (*Photo 67* shows that Nage
stays in the same foot position as in
Photo 66, but actually he should move to
Uke's right side, putting his left foot
alongside Uke's right side to get out of
Uke's way when he grasps Uke's wrist.)
The correct wrist hold is shown in *Photo
67.* At this point, Nage should not grasp
Uke's wrist with his right hand because
he has to switch his right hand position
later. After Nage moves to Uke's right
side, he brings Uke's arm down to the
Nikkyo hand position (*Photo 68*). Nage
continues to hold Uke's wrist with his
left hand. Finally Nage grasps Uke's hand
with his right hand, as shown in *Photo
69,* and as soon as he holds Uke's hand
for Nikkyo, he brings it to his left shoulder. Nage is about to put pressure on
Uke's wrist; his right thumb is on Uke's
thumb and he puts his little finger on the
part where Uke's wrist bends, closing his
right hand tightly. Nage then puts his
left hand on Uke's forearm gently, and
slides it to his right hand (*Photo 70*). It
is easy at this point to lose the position
of the right hand; therefore it is necessary to hold tightly. As Nikkyo is applied,
Uke is forced down (*Photo 71*).

Photo 66

Photo 68

Photo 69

Photo 70

Photo 71

Photo 72   *Photo 73*

Photo 74

Photo 75

KATATORI NIKKYO, *Tenkan* MOVEMENT
Katatori refers to an opponent's shoulder hold. In *Photo 72*, Uke holds Nage's left shoulder so tightly that Nage cannot utilize any Aikido technique unless he first moves to upset Uke's balance. As soon as Uke holds Nage, Nage should move as in *Photo 73*. As Nage moves, if he pulls only his shoulder back, he would lose his balance easily. Nage must leave his shoulder relaxed and move his left hip first, as he withdraws his left foot. At this point, a defender should hit his attacker's face when he steps back; but when you practice, do not hit, just put your fist in front of your opponent's face so that he cannot follow your movement backward. In the illustrations here, it is very important for Nage to put his fist in front of Uke, because he wants Uke to stay away from him as well as to block Uke's left punch. Just after Nage has stepped back, he brings his right hand to Uke's wrist and holds it (*Photo 74*). In *Photo 75*, Nage places himself alongside Uke's right. As he places his left foot next to Uke's right, Nage twists Uke's wrist using his shoulder, and his left hand is ready to hold Uke's wrist. Nage is in this position and is about to apply Nikkyo to Uke (*Photo 76*). *Photo 77* shows the proper hold position for Nage. Nage bends Uke's wrist

Photo 76   *Photo 77*

and elbow the way they bend naturally.
After Uke kneels on the mat, Nage moves
his left hand to Uke's elbow to bring Uke
down flat on the mat; then he pivots as
he pushes Uke's arm down in a circular
movement (*Photos 78, 79,* and *80*). *Photo
81* shows a conclusion to this Nikkyo
technique. Nage kneels and places his
right knee above Uke's shoulder so that
Uke cannot move forward, and forces
Uke's right arm across his back. Putting
his right hand on Uke's elbow, Nage holds
Uke's arm close to his body and his left
hand holds Uke's wrist while he moves
his body in the direction of Uke's head.
Nage must keep his back erect during
this movement.

Photo 78   Photo 79

Photo 80

Photo 81

Photo 82

Photo 84

Photo 83

KATATETORI RYOTE-MOCHI NIKKYO, *Tenkan* MOVEMENT When Uke holds Nage's hand as shown in *Photo 82,* Nage should move before he applies any technique against Uke. Although I have already explained Nage's first movement against this attack, I would like to discuss it again; constant repetition is very important. *Photo 83* shows how Nage experiences difficulty if he depends only on force. If he closes his fingers, as in *Photo 83,* power stops at Uke's hands and Nage's whole arm and shoulder become very tight. This will make Uke resist. If this happens, Nage cannot move at all unless he is much more powerful than Uke.

Photo 84 shows Nage's correct move-

Photo 85

Photo 86

ment: Keeping his shoulder and whole arm relaxed, Nage aproaches Uke, shifting his weight to his right foot. As soon as Nage approaches Uke and gets out of Uke's way, he extends his arm in the direction he is facing, or the direction in which Uke intends to go. Notice that the action is in one direction in *Photo 84*. After Nage shfts his weight to his right foot, he brings his left foot back, and at the same time lifts his right arm. He can do this easily as long as he extends his *ki* enough, because their power joins after Nage places himself in the same direction as Uke (*Photo 85*). Then Nage brings his left foot to the same position where it was before. In other words, he pivots backward, then forward again. On the forward pivot, his left hand grasps Uke's right hand, to hold Uke's hand where it is; he then brings his right hand over Uke's right wrist (*Photo 86*). Before we proceed to *Photo 87*, glance again at *Photo 82* for a comparison. You will notice that Nage returns to his original position. In *Photo 82*, Nage's hand is down and in *Photo 86*, he brings his right hand up to put it over Uke's right arm, which he could not do in the position of *Photo 82*. Then, as shown in *Photos 87* and *88* Nage brings Uke down by putting pressure down on Uke's wrist. This Nikkyo looks different from the others, but it works the same way on Uke's wrist.

Photo 87

Photo 88

MUNE-TSUKI NIKKYO, *Tenkan* MOVE-
MENT   Mune-Tsuki means to thrust at,
or punch, the stomach. In this technique,
Nage applies Nikkyo against the Mune-
Tsuki attack.

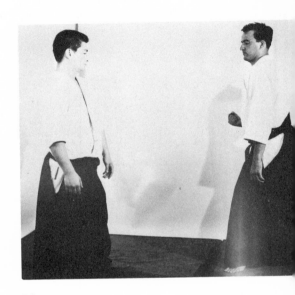

Photo 89

In *Photo 89* Nage stands with his left
foot forward, ready for Uke's right-hand
punch. As Uke punches, Nage must move
straight back with his left foot, as shown
in *Photo 90*. Using his right hand, Nage
catches Uke's fist, guiding the direction of
Uke's punch downward. Nage should not
pull Uke's hand toward himself, as he
may thereby lose his balance. In *Photo
91*, Nage swings Uke's right arm (keeping his own arm straight and relaxed) to
his left shoulder. Stepping to Uke's right
side, Nage brings his left hand to Uke's
wrist. For explanation of *Photos 92* and
93, see the two previous techniques, Katatori Nikkyo and Katatetori Ryote-
Mochi Nikkyo.

Photo 90

Photo 91

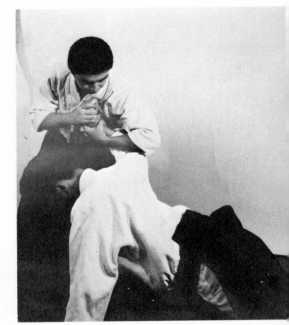

Photo 92

Photo 93

The Sankyo Technique

Sankyo is the third basic "lock" technique of Aikido. It is extremely painful and can be used well in self-defense.

Photo 94 shows the proper way to hold the hand for the application of Sankyo. In this demonstration, Nage is applying Sankyo to Uke's left hand. Nage's right palm should be on the back of Uke's hand and he should close his last three fingers. Nage holds Uke's fingers in his left hand, palm against palm. Nage twists Uke's hand to the right, or toward Uke's body.

Photo 94

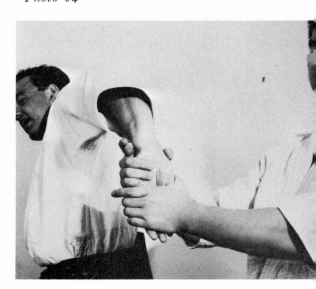

Photo 95

Photo 96

Photo 97

SHOMEN-UCHI SANKYO, *Irimi* MOVE-MENT Shomen-Uchi (a blow to the fore-head) should be received by Nage in the same way described earlier for the Sho-men-Uchi Ikkyo, *Irimi* movement (here see *Photos 95* and *96*). After Nage gets Uke down with the Ikkyo technique (*Photo 97*), Nage applies the Sankyo technique to Uke's wrist. Now, in *Photos 98* and *99* Nage switches his left hand down to Uke's right hand. Nage makes sure that Uke's balance is upset while he changes his hand position (*Photo 100*). Nage moves his right hand to Uke's el-bow, extending both arms downward and twisting Uke's hand with his left hand. The twisting motion must be continued until the technique is finished. With pres-sure on Uke's elbow, Nage should step around with his right foot in front of Uke's arm and head (not shown) guiding Uke straight down to the mat (*Photo 101*). *Photo 102* shows the ending of the Sankyo technique. Nage's inside foot should be under Uke's shoulder. Nage then presses Uke's palm against Nage's thigh, jut above the knee, and shifts his weight to the forward foot, increasing the pressure on Uke's arm.

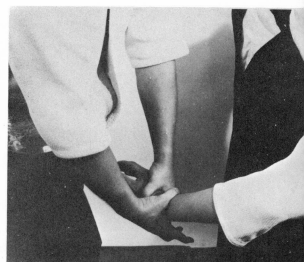

Photo 98   *Photo 99*

Photo 100

Photo 101 Photo 102

 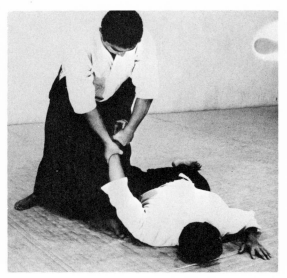

Photo 103

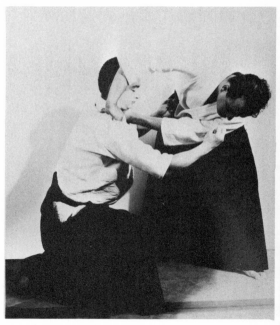

Photo 104

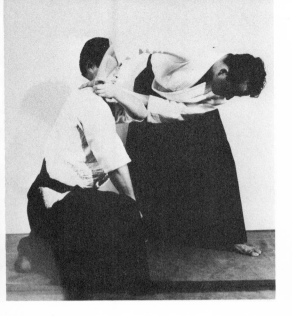

Photo 105

Photo 106

USHIRO-KATATORI SANKYO, *Tenkan* MOVEMENT Ushiro-Katatori refers to an opponent's hold on both shoulders from behind. As shown in *Photo 103*, Uke keeps both arms rigid, so that Nage cannot move backward. There are four directions in which Nage can move: He can move forward, step to the side, go straight down, or pivot in place. Each of these movements has to be executed without pushing Uke back. In this technique, Nage moves to the side and then down.

To get into the position shown in *Photo 104*, Nage puts his right foot to the side to make room for his left foot to step back. As Nage steps back on his left foot, he should put his head down and lower his whole body. Since Nage is stepping all the way behind Uke and Uke is putting pressure on Nage's shoulders, Uke loses his balance when Nage makes this movement. It is as when a person is about to sit on a chair; if somebody pulls the chair back, he cannot stop his action and naturally falls down. In the position shown in *Photo 104*, Nage puts his left knee on the mat, keeping his back straight. If it is not straight, he will lose his balance when Uke attempts to push him down. In *Photo 105*, Nage holds Uke's wrist with his left hand, and Uke's wrist is ready for the application of Sankyo. Even if Uke is still holding Nage's shoulders, Nage does not have to remove Uke's hand. Uke will remove his hand because of pain as Nage stands up (see *Photo 106*). In order to bring Uke down to the mat, Nage swings his left arm down, which puts pressure on Uke's wrist (Sankyo) and places his right hand on Uke's elbow (*Photo 107*). Moving his left foot to Uke's back and bringing Uke's right arm to the direction that Uke's arm points, Nage continues his pivot until Uke is down flat on the mat (*Photo 108*).

Photo 107

Photo 108

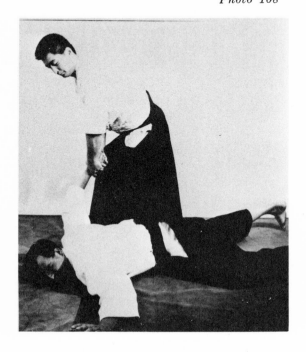

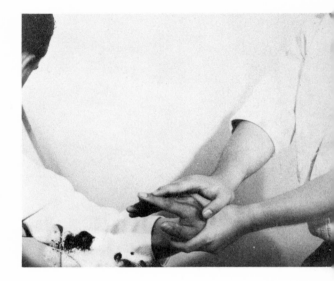

Photo 109

The Kotegaeshi Technique

This is another wrist technique. As shown in *Photo 109*, Nage bends Uke's wrist to the inside and rolls Uke's wrist in the direction that his (Nage's) fingers point.

SHOMEN-UCHI KOTEGAESHI, *Tenkan*
MOVEMENT Nage applies Kotegaeshi
against Uke's Shomen-Uchi (forehead
blow) attack (*Photo 110*). As Uke attacks,

Photo 110

Nage brings his right arm up, but he does
not grasp Uke's wrist (*Photo 111*). While
lifting his arm, Nage places his left foot
to Uke's right side to get out of Uke's
way and slides his left hand from Uke's
shoulder to his wrist and holds it, as
shown in *Photo 112*. Nage then moves his
right foot back to lead Uke around him
(*Photo 113*). He should extend his left
arm, and should not look at Uke. (*Photo
114* is an illustration of Nage's placing
himself in a vulnerable position by pulling Uke's arm toward himself. In this
position, Uke can hit Nage, who has left
himself exposed to Uke's reach.) Notice
in *Photo 113* that Nage keeps Uke's wrist
at waist level and no higher. In order to
keep it that low, Nage must put his left
foot back when he rolls Uke's wrist (*Photo
115*).

I will now explain how to hold Kotegaeshi. Refer to *Photo 113* again. Nage

Photo 111

Photo 112

Photo 113   Photo 114

puts his thumb on the back of Uke's hand and places his other fingers on Uke's wrist; as Nage exerts pressure on Uke's wrist, he puts his right palm on his own left thumb. In *Photo 116,* Uke falls down because of the pain. As soon as Uke falls, Nage should place his right hand inside Uke's elbow, as shown in *Photo 117.* Pushing Uke's elbow toward Uke's face, Nage then walks around Uke's head until he gets in position at Uke's right (*Photo 118*). Keeping Uke's left arm straight, Nage bends Uke's wrist toward Uke's shoulder (*Photo 119*). At the same time, Nage moves Uke's arm forward with his left leg.

Photo 115   *Photo 116*

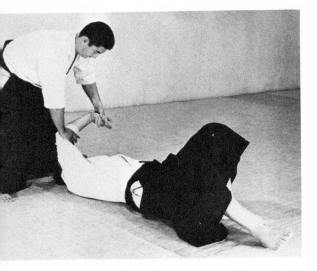

Photo 117

Photo 118

Photo 119

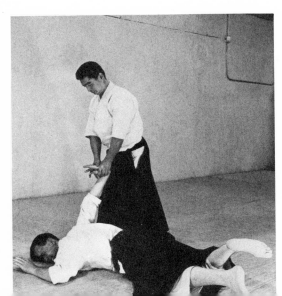

Photo 120

MUNE-TSUKI KOTEGAESHI, *Tenkan* MOVEMENT Nage stands with his right foot forward as Uke punches (*Photo 120*). This movement is the same as Shomen-Uchi Kotegaeshi (*Photos 121* and *122*). Nage also can use the same movement applying Kotegaeshi against a punch to the face, as long as the punch comes in a straight line. In *Photo 123*, it would appear that Uke can deliver a left punch easily to Nage, but actually Nage does not give Uke a chance for such action. As soon as he is in that position, Nage should put pressure on Uke's wrist so that Uke is forced down (*Photo 124*).

Photo 121   *Photo 122*

 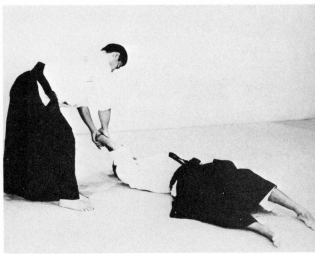

Photo 123   *Photo 124*

KATATE-TORI RYOTE-MOCHI KOTEGAE-SHI, *Tenkan* MOVEMENT Uke grasps Nage's wrist and arm with both hands (*Photo 125*). Nage pivots and lifts Uke's arms (*Photos 126* and *127;* note that *Photos 126* and *127* show the same position but from opposite sides). As he does so, Nage puts his right foot back as far

Photo 126

Photo 125

as he can, at the same time swinging his right arm down, fully extended, and placing his left hand in the Kotegaeshi position (*Photo 128*). It is easy for Nage to swing his right arm down if he keeps his arm relaxed. After he swings his arm down to hold Kotegaeshi, Nage should put Uke's wrist directly in front of his body. In *Photo 129,* Nage puts his left foot back to make room for Uke to fall. Uke is forced to fall in exactly that spot from which Nage moved his left foot. Nage should keep Uke's wrist low and should push Uke's wrist straight down while he is turning his body (*Photo 130*).

Photo 127

Photo 128

Photo 129

Photo 130

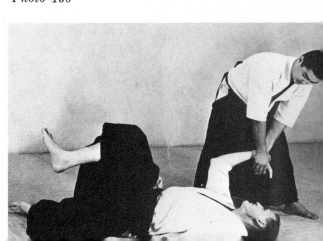

Photo 131

Photo 132

USHIRO-TEKUBI-TORI KOTEGAESHI Ushiro-Tekubi-Tori refers to an opponent's hold on both wrists from behind. In this demonstration, Uke pulls Nage's wrists upward and toward himself (*Photo 131*). Because his arms are lifted, Nage will feel pain and find it difficult to use force, as shown in *Photo 132*. Nage should keep his shoulders and arms relaxed so that he will not receive Uke's power. Even if Uke uses great strength on Nage, if Nage remains relaxed, force will have no effect on him (with the exception of locks against his joints).

Before Nage makes any movement, he should bend his wrist forward in the direction he intends to lead Uke's power. Since Uke is holding Nage very tightly, it is difficult for Nage to bring his hands to his sides. However, if he keeps his shoulders relaxed, Nage can move his body to his wrists. In *Photo 133*, Nage bends forward, and his hip moves back naturally to his wrists. (As he bends, Nage should not do anything with his arms but just leave them relaxed. If he tries to use his arms, he cannot even bow.) As Nage straighten up, he brings his arms up in the direction that his fingers point (at this time they should point up). Nage can only move his arms by starting an upward curling motion with his hands,

Photo 133

Photo 134

until his hands are a few inches in front of his eyes. At this time he should reverse the position of his hands to point his fingers downward, the direction he intends to lead Uke. At this stage, Nage keeps his elbows down so that he can support Uke's weight and pressure (*Photo 134*). From this position, Nage twists his hip to his left side and moves his left foot in the same direction. As he twists his hip, his left arm comes down to remain in front of him, and his right arm is ready to reach Uke's wrist to hold Kotegaeshi (*Photo 135*). In *Photo 136*, Nage is holding Uke's wrist and applying Kotegaeshi. *Photo 137* shows the conclusion of this technique.

Photo 135   *Photo 136*

The Kokyu-Nage Technique

The name Kokyu-Nage is used for various Aikido techniques. They are primarily employed as throwing techniques without the application of pressure on any joint. Kokyu-Nage requires strong *ki*, fine timing, and good balance.

Photo 137

SHOMEN-UCHI KOKYU-NAGE In the Shomen-Uchi Kokyu-Nage technique, Uke attacks Nage with Shomen-Uchi (striking at the forehead), and Nage stands with his right foot forward to resist Uke's right-hand blow (*Photo 138*). As Uke comes toward him, Nage brings his right hand straight up and brings his left foot behind, in the same manner as the initial movements of Shomen-Uchi Kotegaeshi.

Photo 138

He then puts his left hand on the back of Uke's neck (*Photo 139*). He does not grasp Uke's wrist with his right hand, but cuts downward as he pivots to his right side from the position of *Photo 139*. (*Photo 140* shows the position after the pivot.) As he pivots, Nage uses his left hand to bring Uke's neck to his right shoulder. Nage should keep his right arm straight, as shown in *Photo 140·* He will then turn his fingers toward Uke's face, where he will place his arm in the next motion. In *Photo 141*, Nage raises Uke's body. At the same time that Nage raises

Photo 139

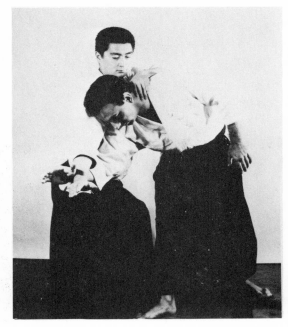

Photo 140

Uke, he should turn his face and twist his hip in his intended direction. Thus Nage concentrates all his *ki,* using his entire body.

Raising Uke is relatively easy to accomplish now because Uke will try to lift himself to regain his balance. *Photo 142* was taken from the opposite direction of *Photo 141.* Nage's left hand remains on the back of Uke's neck and his right fingers still point down. He has enough room to put his right foot forward because he twisted his hip when he raised Uke. After Uke loses balance, Nage can easily put his right foot forward. Nage should not step until Uke loses balance, because Uke could then throw Nage. Notice that Nage's right hand is pointed downward in *Photos 143* and *144.*

Photo 141   *Photo 142*

Photo 143

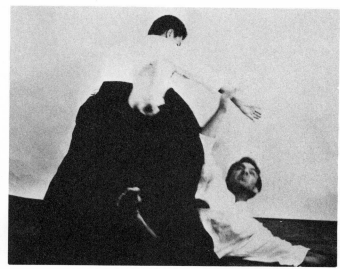

Photo 144

Photo 145

Photo 146

Photo 147

Photo 148

YOKOMEN-UCHI KOKYU-NAGE TECH-NIQUE A   As Uke delivers his blow to the left side of Nage's face (*Photo 145*), Nage blocks the blow with his left hand and brings his left foot back. The movements of *Photos 146* and *147* have been explained in the Yokomen-Uchi Shiho-Nage technique.

In *Photo 147*, Uke has lost his balance because Nage made a wide move, enabling Nage to complete the form. To repeat, Nage should make his first move as wide as he can. As shown in *Photo 147*, Nage should stand straight after he makes his first move against Uke's attack in order to anticipate Uke's reaction. Moving his left hand to Uke's neck, Nage is about to put his left foot behind Uke's back (*Photo 148*). Notice that, in *Photos 149* and *150*, Nage extends his right arm. This helps to make Nage's movement wide and smooth. The steps shown in *Photos 148* through

Photo 149

Photo 150

150 must be executed simultaneously. In *Photo 151*, Nage removes his right hand from its former position at Uke's wrist and raises it to encircle Uke's neck. At this point, as described in the last technique, Nage should place his left hand on Uke's neck and then press Uke's neck to his right shoulder in order to prevent Uke's escape. Stepping forward on his right foot, Nage drops Uke to the mat (*Photo 152*).

Photo 151

Photo 152

Photo 153

YOKOMEN-UCHI KOKYU-NAGE, TECH-
NIQUE B Uke delivers a blow to the left
side of Nage's face (*Photo 153*). As Nage
steps back, he cuts Uke's right arm down
with both his arms (*Photo 154*). Nage
then extends both arms. Pivoting slightly
to his left side, Nage continues to cut
downward as in *Photo 155*. He may hold
Uke's wrist lightly with his left hand.
Nage should always keep his hands directly in front of him. As Nage puts
pressure on Uke's right arm, he should
try to send his power (his *ki*) all the way
down to the mat (and not stop it by
concentrating only on Uke's arm). As
Nage pivots to his left side, he should
rest his left knee on the mat to maintain
balance while he completes the motion
(*Photo 156*).

Photo 154

Photo 155

Photo 156

KATATE-TORI RYOTE-MOCHI KOKYU-NAGE Uke holds Nage's right arm tightly with both hands (*Photo 157*). Nage extends his right arm and sends his *ki* downward (*Photo 158*). Uke will lose balance because he is holding Nage's arm very tightly and all of his power is concentrated on it. Leading Uke to his right side with his right hand, Nage should bring his left foot forward until it is almost behind Uke. At the same time, Nage swings his left arm vigorously and brings it to Uke's neck as shown in *Photo 159*. Nage's right arm should remain straight.

Photo 157

In *Photo 160*, Nage brings his right foot back, pivoting after he has put his left foot behind Uke, and brings Uke's neck to his right shoulder. Nage's right arm is still extended as he brings his weight low, bending his knees. Following *Photo 160*, Nage raises Uke, but now both of Uke's arms are on Nage's right hand. Nage can-

 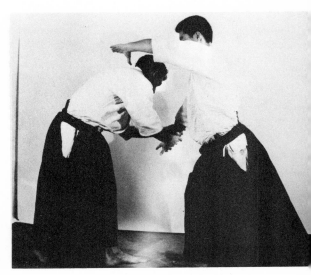

Photo 158   *Photo 159*

not push his right arm straight toward Uke's shoulder. It is obvious that if he does, he will meet Uke's power and find difficulty. Instead, he brings his arm straight up without forcing Uke to bend his arms. After he has risen completely, Nage points his right fingers downward and is ready to push Uke down (*Photo 161*). As Nage brings his right arm up and then down in a circular motion, he twists his hip in the same direction (*Photo 162*).

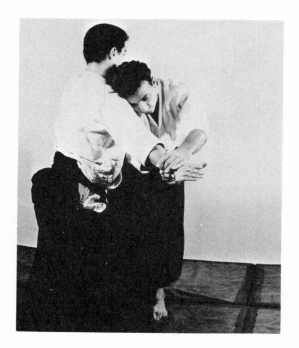

Photo 160

Photo 161

Photo 162

The Koshi-Nage Technique

The hip throws in Aikido should be practiced only by advanced students and with an instructor. In any hip throw, an opponent will feel a shock when he is thrown to the mat, and if he does not fall properly, he may suffer serious injury.

KATATE-TORI RYOTE-MOCHI KOSHI-NAGE In this hip throw, Uke holds Nage's right arm in both hands (*Photo 163*). Nage pivots to Uke's left side and brings his right arm up to lift Uke and to stretch Uke's body upward (*Photo 164*). Thereupon, he places his hip under Uke's and then brings his arm down, pointing his fingers to the mat as shown in *Photo*

165. Nage should be in a semicrouched position with his legs bent from the knees. His body should be touching Uke. To throw Uke from his back, Nage retrieves his right arm (which Uke has been holding), brings it under to his left side, and straightens his legs from their former bent position (*Photo 166*).

Photo 163

Photo 164

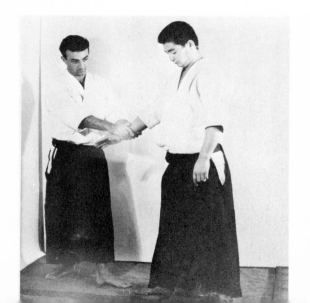

Photo 165

Photo 166

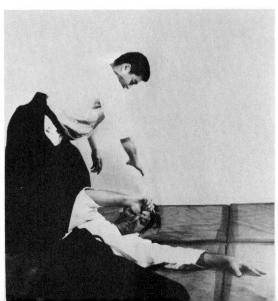

Photo 167

Photo 168

USHIRO-TEKUBI-TORI KOSHI-NAGE Uke holds both of Nage's wrists from behind and Nage bends his wrists, as shown in Photo 167. Nage brings both arms forward and then straightens up to eye level. As Nage's arms pass his face, he turns his arm over to point his fingers down *(Photo 168)*. Nage then bends his upper body to his left and takes his head out from under Uke's arm, twisting his hips to the right but keeping his feet still *(Photo 169)*. As Nage lowers himself, he swings both arms to the left, pointing his fingers in the same direction that he intends to throw Uke. Of course, Nage must bend both knees evenly at this time *(Photo 170)*. If he does not, he will lose his balance easily, because he will receive Uke's weight on the lowest side of his body. Continuing to swing his arms to his left side, Nage straightens his knees *(Photo 171)*.

Photo 169

Photo 170

Photo 171

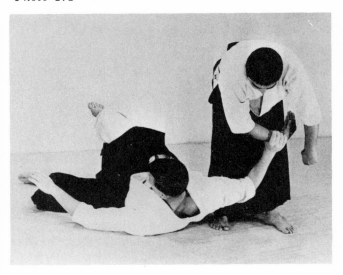

Photo 173

Photo 172

USHIRO-KUBISHIME KOSHI-NAGE Uke chokes Nage from behind (*Photo 172*). As soon as Uke starts to apply his choke hold, Nage pulls his chin in and puts his hand on Uke's right arm *(Photo 173)*. Nage should relax his whole body and concentrate on his one-point, while pressing Uke's right arm to his body with *ki*. At this time, if Nage tells himself that there is an iron stick in his body from head to foot (do not misunderstand, he should not make his body stiff, but should stay relaxed), Uke cannot bend Nage's body backward. In order to throw Uke over his back, Nage brings his head down sharply, almost touching his own knee (*Photo 174*). *Photos 175* and *176* show the conclusion of this technique.

Photo 174

Photo 175

Photo 176

Photo 178

Photo 177

RYOTE-TORI KOSHI-NAGE Uke holds both of Nage's wrists with both hands *(Photo 177)*. Nage should bring his left arm down toward Uke's feet, and his right arm goes up, grasping Uke's wrist *(Photo 178)*. At the same time, Nage twists his hips to the right. Then, putting his left foot between Uke's feet, Nage extends his right arm to lift Uke *(Photo 179)*. As soon as Nage is under Uke's body, he swings his right arm down and straightens his knees, which he has bent to get into a low, strong position *(Photo 180)*. *Photo 181* shows the conclusion of this technique.

Photo 179

Photo 180

Photo 181

Nage-Wasa (Throwing) Techniques

I have already explained some throwing forms (Kokyu-Nage and Koshi-Nage). I would now like to describe four additional Aikido throwing techniques.

Photo 182

Photo 183

TENCHI-NAGE   Uke holds Nage's wrists. Nage has his left foot forward (Photo 182). Nage points the fingers of his left hand down and slides his left foot to Uke's right side. Photo 183 shows the next series of movements: As Nage slides, he shifts his left arm forward (fingers pointing down) and should keep Uke's right arm straight. Nage's right arm should be kept relaxed and his elbow comes down as he moves toward Uke with the fingers of his right hand pointing up.

If Nage stiffens his right arm and tries to push Uke back, he is unlikely to get near Uke, because his rigid arm forces Uke to step back. Nage should remain low when he slides. As shown in Photo 184, Nage then steps forward on his right foot as he brings his right arm straight up. Then, as his right foot lands on the mat, Nage should turn his right hand down to bring Uke down, while his left arm is still moving forward and down (Photo 185), as he finishes the movement (Photo 186).

Photo 184

Photo 185

Photo 186

Photo 187

MUNE-TSUKI KAITEN-NAGE Uke attacks with a straight right-hand punch to Nage's stomach *(Photo 187)*. Nage shifts his left foot to Uke's right side, twisting his hips to his left, and swings his left arm down on Uke's punching arm to act as a block and also to bring Uke low. At the same time, Nage's right arm is about to reach Uke's neck, which also brings Uke low (see *Photo 188*). As soon as Nage touches Uke's neck with his right hand, he brings Uke's neck down and simultaneously brings his left arm up, holding Uke's right arm *(Photo 189)*. Nage also twists his hips to his right in the direction Uke is heading, and pushes Uke's right arm forward, after raising it high. Nage's right arm is still pushing Uke's head down. *Photo 190* shows the throw.

Photo 188

Photo 189

Photo 190

USHIRO-KUBISHIME KOKYU-NAGE Holding Nage's right wrist from behind with his right hand, Uke chokes Nage with his left arm. Nage bends his right wrist to bring Uke's right arm up as shown in *Photo 191*. (As in the choke hold described earlier, Nage must pull his chin in as soon as Uke starts to choke him.) After Nage brings his right arm up to his head *(Photo 192),* he brings it over his head and down by the left side of his face and grasps Uke's right arm, which has been holding Nage's right wrist to his own body. As Nage brings his right arm down, he moves his body to the right (he cannot move to the left; that would increase the pressure on his throat), and brings his left arm up straight to lift Uke's weight. Nage is then in the position shown in *Photo 193*. Because Uke's weight is on Nage's left arm, Uke falls when Nage steps forward on his left foot and bends his body downward (it is important that Nage's left leg be bent at this point). As Nage bends his body, he also brings his left arm down to escape Uke *(Photo 194).*

Photo 191   *Photo 192*

Photo 193

Photo 194

Aikido Techniques against Knife Attacks

After practicing the Aikido techniques shown earlier, one can apply them against knife attacks. I would like to demonstrate some of these applied against different attacks.

1. In this demonstration, Uke attacks the left side of Nage's face (*Photo 195*). Nage uses the same movement and technique as Yokomen-Uchi Ikkyo, *tenkan* movement, except for the way he holds Uke's wrist (*Photo 196*), and the ending (*Photos 201* and *202*)· As Nage slides to Uke's right side at the beginning of this movement, Nage should be careful not to be in the position shown in *Photo 197*, especially when Uke has a knife. Since Uke attacks with a knife, Nage had better take it from him. After Nage gets Uke down (*Photo 201*), he lifts Uke's elbow and brings Uke's wrist across Uke's body to put pressure on Uke's wrist as shown in *Photo 202*. Uke feels pain, so he cannot retain the knife.

Photo 195

Photo 196

Photo 197

Photo 198

Photo 199

Photo 200

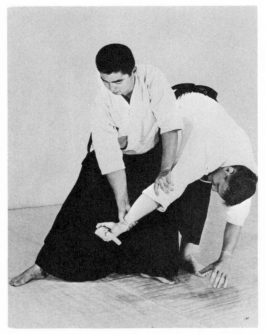

Photo 201   *Photo 202*

 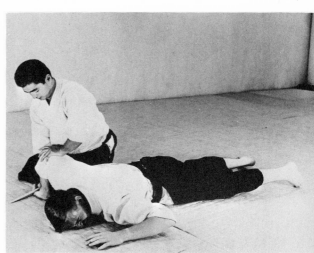

2. In this demonstration, Uke holds a knife under Nage's chin. Nage will be inviting further attack if he merely moves backward *(Photo 203)*. Nage applies the Kotegaeshi technique and takes the knife from Uke. *Photo 204* shows the key part of this technique. As Nage twists his hips to the right, he pushes out with his left hand, extending Uke's right arm and holding the latter's wrist for Kotegaeshi *(Photos 204 and 205)*. *Photo 206* is from a different angle than *Photo 205*; Nage has already put his right foot back, and then puts his left foot back to apply Kotegaeshi *(Photos 207 and 208)*.

Photo 203

Photo 204

Photo 205

Photo 206

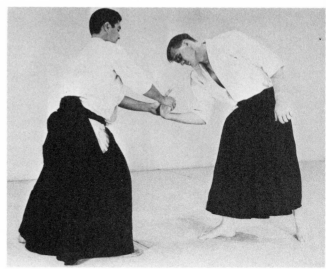

Photo 207

Photo 208

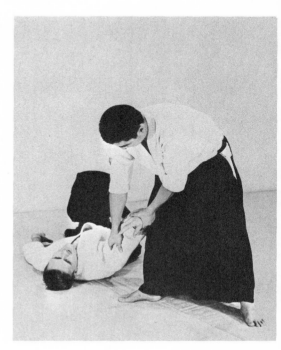

3. In this demonstration Uke attacks Nage's stomach with a knife *(Photo 209)*. Nage again applies Kotegaeshi, using the Mune-Tsuki Kotegaeshi movement. As Uke attacks in a straight line, Nage moves to Uke's right side and catches Uke's wrist with his left hand *(Photo 210)* for Kotegaeshi *(Photos 211 and 212)*.

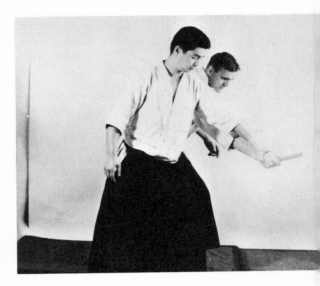

Photo 209

Photo 2

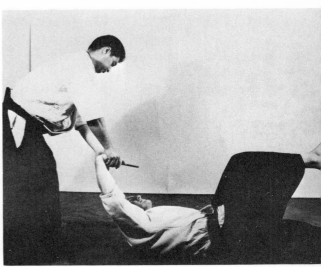

Photo 211

Photo 212

4. In this demonstration, Uke swings a knife from his left side *(Photo 213)*. As Uke swings his right arm from his left side at Nage's stomach, Nage places his left foot behind Uke, cutting Uke's right arm down as shown in *Photo 214*. This movement is the same in Shomen-Uchi Kokyu-Nage. Nage puts his left hand on the back of Uke's neck to lead him down *(Photo 215)*. Nage can apply two final movements from the one shown in *Photo 215*. *Photo 216* shows the same concluding motion as that used in the Shomen-Uchi Kokyu-Nage technique. To achieve the position shown in *Photo 217*, from that shown in *Photo 215*, Nage slides his left foot behind Uke, choking him with his left arm and locking Uke's right elbow as indicated in *Photo 217*.

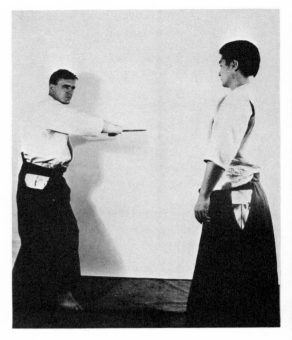

Photo 213

Photo 214

Photo 215

conclusion

The reader will note throughout the book that there have been constant repetitions of most facets of Aikido. Many photographs of certain demonstrations have been repeated. The purpose of this has been to give strong accent to a number of the more important phases of Aikido.

In conclusion, I wish to review briefly and to stress again two key factors relating to this martial art:

First, exercise care at all times in practice sessions. Make certain that neither you nor your "opponent" utilizes force in the practice of the techniques. It is the improper application of force by beginners that can result in injury.

Second, the basic importance of Aikido is to learn the art of self-defense. Within the techniques of Aikido, there are deeper meanings and philosophies. If practiced properly, Aikido can be an instrument by which one's mind, spirit, and emotions—as well as his body—can evolve into one serene entity.